ISBN 978-1-330-67505-2
PIBN 10090744

1 MONTH OF
FREE
READING

at
www.ForgottenBooks.com

By purchasing this book you are eligible for one month membership to ForgottenBooks.com, giving you unlimited access to our entire collection of over 1,000,000 titles via our web site and mobile apps.

To claim your free month visit:
www.forgottenbooks.com/free90744

English
Français
Deutsche
Italiano
Español
Português

www.forgottenbooks.com

Mythology Photography **Fiction**
Fishing Christianity **Art** Cooking
Essays Buddhism Freemasonry
Medicine **Biology** Music **Ancient**
Egypt Evolution Carpentry Physics
Dance Geology **Mathematics** Fitness
Shakespeare **Folklore** Yoga Marketing
Confidence Immortality Biographies
Poetry **Psychology** Witchcraft
Electronics Chemistry History **Law**
Accounting **Philosophy** Anthropology
Alchemy Drama Quantum Mechanics
Atheism Sexual Health **Ancient History**
Entrepreneurship Languages Sport
Paleontology Needlework Islam
Metaphysics Investment Archaeology
Parenting Statistics Criminology
Motivational

A Girl's Student Days and After

By
JEANNETTE MARKS, M. A.
(*Wellesley*)

With an Introduction by
MARY EMMA WOOLLEY, LL. D.
President of Mt. Holyoke College

New York   Chicago   Toronto
Fleming H. Revell Company
London   and   Edinburgh

New York: 158 Fifth Avenue
Chicago: 125 North Wabash Ave.
Toronto: 25 Richmond Street, W.
London: 21 Paternoster Square
Edinburgh: 100 Princes Street

Inscribed

to

MARY EMMA WOOLLEY, LL. D.

Introduction

THE school and college girl is an important factor in our life to-day. Around her revolve all manner of educational schemes, to her are open all kinds of educational opportunities. There was never an age in which so much thought was expended upon her, or so much interest felt in her development.

There are many articles written and many speeches delivered on the responsibility of parents and teachers—it may not be amiss occasionally to turn the shield and show that some of the responsibility rests upon the girl herself. After all, she is the determining factor, for buildings and equipment, courses and teachers accomplish little without her coöperation.

It is difficult for the "new girl," whether in school or college, to realize the extent to which the success of her school life depends upon herself. In a new environment, surrounded by what seem to her "multitudes" of new faces, obliged to meet larger demands under strange and untried conditions, she is quite likely to go to the other extreme and exaggerate her own insignificance. Sometimes she is fortunate enough to have an older sister or friend to help her steer her bark through these untried waters, but generally she must find her own bearings.

To such a girl, the wise hints in the chapters which follow this introduction are invaluable, giving an insight into the meaning of fair-play in the classroom as well as on the athletic field; the relation between physical well-being and academic success; the difference between the social life that is *re*-creative and that which is "*nerves*-creative"; the significance of loyalty to the school and to the home; the way in which school days determine to a large degree the days that come after. These, and many other suggestions, wise and forceful, I commend not only to the new girl, but also to the "old girl" who would make her school and college days count for more both while they last and as preparation for the work that is to follow.

MARY E. WOOLLEY.

Mt. Holyoke College,
South Hadley, Massachusetts.

CONTENTS

A Word to the Wise

WE train for basket-ball, golf, tennis or for whatever sport we have the most liking. Is there any reason why we should not use the same intelligence in the approach to our general school life? Is there any reason why we should make an obstacle race, however good and amusing exercise that may be, out of *all* our school life? We don't expect to win a game with a sprained wrist or ankle, and there really is no reason why we should plan to sprain the back of school or college life by avoidable mistakes.

The writer believes in the girl who has the capacity for making mistakes,—that headlong, energetic spirit which blunders all too easily. But the writer knows how much those mistakes hurt and how much energy might be saved for a life that, with just a pinch less of blunder, might be none the less savoury. School and college are no place for vocal soloists, and after some of us have sung so sweetly and so long at home, with every one saying, "Just hear Mary sing, isn't it wonderful!" it is rather trying, you know, to go to a place where vocal solos are not popular. And we wish some one—at least I did—had told us all about this fact as well as other facts of school life. Anyway it should be a comfort to have a book lying on the table in our school or college room, or at home, which will tell us why Mary, after having been a famous soloist at home made a failure or a great success in chorus work at school. Such a book is something like having a loaded gun in readiness for the robber. We may never use the shotgun or the book but they are there, with the reassuring sense of shot in the locker.

It is something, is it not, to have a little book which will tell you how to get into school and how to get out (for at times there seem to be difficulties in both these directions)—in short, to tell you something of many things : your first year at school or college, your part in the school life, the friendships you will make, your study and how to work in it, the pleasure and right kind of spirit involved in work, the quiet times, as well as the jolly times, out-of-doors, your summers and how to spend them, what the school has tried to do for you ; and, as you go out into the world, some of the aspects, whether you are to be wife, secretary or teacher, of the work which you will do. Of one thing you may be certain ; that behind every sentence of this little book is experience, that here are only those opinions of which experience has made a good, wholesome zwieback.

I wish to take this opportunity to thank my friend, Mrs. Belle Kellogg Towne, editor of *The Girls' Companion* and *Young People's Weekly*, Chicago, for her coöperation in allowing me to use half the material in this little book ; also Dr. C. R. Blackall, of Philadelphia.

Camp Runway.   J. M.

I

THE IDEAL FRESHMAN

FRESHMAN year, the beginning year, the year of new experiences, new delights, new work, new friends, new surroundings ; the year that may mean much to a girl, that may answer some of the questions that have lain long in heart and mind, that will surely reveal her more clearly to herself, that may make her understand others better and help her to guess something of the riddle of the years to come!

What has the student done to get ready for this year? If she were going camping she would know that certain things were necessary to make the expedition a success. With what excitement and pleasure, what thoughts of jolly camp-fires, deep, sweet-smelling forests, and long days afoot, she would prepare everything. She would not let any one else do this for her, for that would mean losing too much of the fun. But the *freshman year*, what about the thinking and planning for that, also an expedition into a new world, and a veritable adventure of a vast deal more importance than a few days or weeks of camping? Would she enter forests upon whose trees the camp-fires throw many shadows, follow the stream that cleaves its way through the woods, go along the runway of deer or caribou or moose, with a mind to all intents and purposes a blank? No, her mind would be vivid with thoughts and interests.

With the same keen attention should she enter the new year at school or college, and as she passes through it, thinking about all that comes to her, she will find it growing less and less difficult and more and more friendly. She will consider what the freshman year is to be like, think of what sorts of girls she is to meet and make friends with, what the work will be, what she may expect in good times from this new adventure, and, thoughtful about it all, make the minimum of mistakes and get the maximum of benefit.

Here come some of the girls who are entering school and college with her—bright-haired, dark-haired, rosy or pale, tall and thin, fat and short, clever and average, desirable and undesirable,—in fact, all sorts and conditions of girls. Who is to be the leader of them all? She is the *ideal freshman*, a nice, well-set-up girl who does not think too much of herself, who is not self-conscious, and who does not forget for what she is sent to school. Despite the temptations of school life she uses her days wisely and well. She does not isolate herself, for she sees the plan and value of the recreative side of school-days. She is already laying the foundations for a successful, useful, normal existence, establishing confidence at the outset and not handicapping herself through her whole course by making people lose their faith in her. Our *ideal freshman* may be the girl who is to do distinguished work; she may be the student who does her best; and because it is her best, the work, though not brilliant, is distinguished by virtue of her effort. She may be the girl who is to make a happy home life through her poise and earnestness and common sense. Whoever she is, in any event in learning to do her best she is winning nine-tenths of the battle of a successful career. It is she, attractive, able, earnest, with the "fair-play" or team-play spirit in all she does, true to herself and to others, whom every school wants, whose unconscious influence is so great in building up the morale of any school. Mark this girl and follow her, for she is worthy of your hero worship.

This is the girl who goes into school in much the same spirit that she would enter upon a larger life. She is not a prig and she is not a dig, but she knows there are responsibilities to be met and she meets them. She expects to have to think about the new conditions in which she finds herself and to adjust herself to them, and she does it. She knows the meaning of the team-play spirit and she takes her place quietly on the team, one among many, and both works and plays with respect for the rights and positions of others. It is in the temper of the words sometimes stamped upon the coins of our country—*E Pluribus Unum*—that she makes a success of her school life. She knows that not only is our country bigger than any one of its states, but also that every school is bigger than any one of its members whether teacher or student. In a small family at home conditions have been more or less made for her, just as they are for other girls. Yet she knows that the school life is complicated and complex, and it is impossible for her to feel neglected where a more self-centred or spoiled girl fails to see that in this new life she is called upon to play a minor part but nevertheless a part upon which the school must rely for its *esprit de corps*. She goes with ease from the somewhat unmethodical life of the home to the highly organized routine of the school because she understands the meaning of the word " team-play." She has the coöperative spirit.

Yet there are other girls, too, in this school which the freshman is entering. There is the student who errs on the side of leading too workaday a life, and in so doing has lost something of the buoyancy and breadth and "snap" which would make her associations and her work fresher and more vigorous. "The Grind," she has been called, and if she recognize herself in this sketch, let her take care to reach out for a bigger and fuller life than she is leading. And there is, too, the selfish student whose " class-spirit " is self-spirit; and the girl who is not selfish but who uses herself up in too many interests, dramatic, athletic, society, philanthropic and in a dozen others. She is probably over-conscientious, a good girl in every way, but in doing too much she loses sight of the real aim of her school life. To these must be added another student,— the freshman who skims the surface, and is, when she gets out, where she was when she entered—no, not quite so far along, for she has slipped back. She is selfish, relying upon the patience and burden-bearing capacity of her father and mother, as well as the school.

No doubt every girl would meet her obligations squarely if she realized what was the underlying significance of the freshman year; the school life would surely be approached with a conscientious purpose. What a girl gets in school will much depend upon what she has to give. No girl is there simply to have a good time or merely to learn things out of books. Nor is she there to fill in the interim between childhood and young womanhood, when one will go into society, another marry, and a third take up some wage-earning career. No, she is there to carry life forward in the deepest, truest sense; and the longer she can have to get an education and to make the best of the opportunities of school and college life, the richer and fuller her after-years will be. Both middle life and old age will be deeper and stronger. Let us think about these girls, let us think about what it means to be a freshman, and so lessen our difficulties and increase our pleasures; let us have a big conception,—a large ideal always at heart—of what the *first year* should be, and beginning well we shall be the more likely to end well.

II

THE GIRL AND THE SCHOOL

INSIDE school or college the girl is in several ways responsible for the atmosphere. Merely in her conversation she can be of service or dis-service. It may be simply a good joke which she is telling, but if the joke misrepresents the school she will, perhaps, do lasting harm. If she is hypercritical—and there is nothing so contagious as criticism—she influences people in the direction of her thought; she sets a current of criticism in motion. A student frequently gives vent to an opinion that is only half-baked—it is well, by the way, to make zwieback of all our opinions before we pass them around as edible—about courses and instructors. She does not realize that some opinions to be worth anything must be the result of a long process of baking, that a nibble from the corner of a four months' or nine months' course will not, however understandingly it may be Fletcherized, tell you whether the course is going to be fruit cake, meringue or common soda crackers. She may think that she herself is so unimportant that what she says can't matter, or she may not mean what she says and be merely letting off steam. Nevertheless her influence is exerted. Some one showed an old lady, who had never been known to say anything in the least critical of any human being, the picture of a very fat man prominent in public life. She looked at it a moment, and then said sweetly : " My, isn't he plump !" If only there were more old and young ladies like that dear soul !

There is another kind of conversation which may not be ill-natured and yet does harm. Idle gossiping, talking about things that are not worth while or speculating about affairs which are not our business and of which we know little or nothing. Akin to this is fashionably slangy conversation concerning the latest thing in books, magazine articles, trivial plays. For even the "tone" of school or college conversation a student is responsible. She can make her school seem cheap or cultivated. The remarks which visitors overhear as they go from room to room or from building to building are likely to indicate the "tone" of an institution. A catalogue may say all it pleases about a school but in the end the school is judged by the women it educates and sends out, even as a tree is known by its fruit. Cultivated, strong women are worth more in advertisement than all the printed material in the world, however laudatory.

When a girl has received everything her Alma Mater has to give, she has no right to be untrue to its fundamental aims and ideals, or to misrepresent it in any way, either by what she says or by her own behaviour. Every student in a large institution is in a sense a pensioner. No student can pay for what is given to her. Is it not a poor return for her to be reflecting dishonour rather than honour upon her school?

There is a certain social selfishness in the way some students take their opportunities for granted without realizing that there are thousands and hundreds of thousands of girls who would give all that they possess for a tithe of such riches. Also, because of the sacrifice which is being made for them at home girls are selfish in taking their school or college life carelessly. The school has to bear much of the responsibility for the individual failure. But of this the student who is failing rarely thinks. Parents hold an institution to blame if it does not do for their child what they expect it to do, when it may be the girl who is at fault.

In the use she makes of her portion of inheritance, in the gift the school bestows on the student, there is a large social question involved. The school gives her of its wealth, the result of the accumulation of years and of the civic or philanthropic spirit of many men and women. This, if the girl's sense of responsibility is what it should be, she feels bound to increase and hand on. It is the old *noblesse oblige* under new conditions of privilege.

While she is still in school the girl discharges part of this obligation by realizing what is best for her school as an institution. A college or a big school is no place for vocal soloists. Its life is the life of an orchestra, of many instruments playing together. The student's sense of responsibility is shown by her attitude towards the corporate government and administration of the school. Instead of regarding the laws of her school as natural enemies, chafing against them, making fun of them or evading them if possible, she has a duty in fulfilling them. The consciousness of this responsibility is the very heart and soul of the student self-government movement, for it recognizes not only the obligation placed upon its members by an institution, but also the wide influence one girl may have on others. Student government knows that upper class girls can determine the spirit of the under classes. Even looking at the matter from the lightest point of view, respectful and law-abiding ways are always well-bred ways.

When a student becomes an alumna she can discharge a large part of her great responsibility by realizing that it is not any longer so much a question of what her school can give her as of what she can give to her school. One thing she can always give it— that is, kindly judgment. And she can acknowledge that her ideas of what her Alma Mater is after her own school-days may not be correct. The school, sad to say, is sometimes placed in the position of the kindly old farmer who, hearing others call a certain man a liar, said: "Waal now, I wouldn't say he wuz a *liar*. That's a bit harsh. I'd say he handled the truth mighty careless-like." Schools find that some of their alumnæ handle the truth mighty careless-like.

While she is still a student a girl's service to her school lies largely in her daily work, the mental muscle she puts into all that she does in the classroom and studies out of it. If because of her and a multiple of many girls like her, the college does not possess that *sine qua non* of all the higher mental life, an intellectual atmosphere, it is the student's and her multiple's fault. "You may lead a horse to water but you cannot make it drink," may be an old adage, but it would be hard to improve upon it. You may set before students a veritable Thanksgiving feast of things intellectual, but if they have no eagerness, no appetite for them, the feast remains untouched. Energy and hunger of the mind, not the anxious hosts, will in the end decide whether that feast is or is not to be eaten.

The school considers not only scholarship but also the sum of all that it is, its culture, its attainment, its moral force, as these elements are expressed in its living members, its students and its teachers—in short, its idealism. Idealism is having one's life governed by ideals, and an ideal is a perfect conception of that which is good, beautiful and true. If the girl's life is not governed by ideals, how, then, can the school hope to have its idealism live or grow? Frequently students think of the ideals of college or school as of something outside themselves, more or less intangible, with which they may or may not be concerned. Students cannot do their institution a greater injury than by harbouring such a thought, for if their sense of responsibility will only make the idea of the school personal, then indeed will the school be like that house upon which the rains descended and the winds blew but it fell not, for it was founded upon a rock.

III

FRIENDSHIPS

HOMESICKNESS and friendships, how much and how vivid a part they play in the first year, or years, of school life! An old coloured physician was asked about a certain patient who was very ill. " I'll tell you de truf," was the reply. " Widout any perception, Phoebe Pamela may die and she may get well; dere's considerable danger bofe ways." I will tell you one truth about the first year of school life: friends there will surely be, and homesickness there is likely to be,—there is " considerable danger both ways."

Even if a girl has never been away from home before, it is possible that she will not suffer from homesickness. It is probable, however, that the new surroundings in which the girl finds herself, and the separation from those who are the centre of her personal life, will bring on an attack of this most painful malady. It takes time to fit comfortably into the new surroundings, and meanwhile everything is strange. Homesickness is not to be laughed at, but it must be less deadly, less fatal than some people think it, or there would not be so many recoveries. Girls often weep when they enter school, and then after the long dreary years are really over, lived through, and the poor forlorn freshman is metamorphosed into the senior, they weep again. Is it not strange that these seniors who wept on entering school should weep also when leaving it? It looks in the end as if Phoebe Pamela were sure to get well. Yet the effort to get well requires a fine effort at self-control,—an effort every girl is the better for making, although it may take everything plucky in a girl to "back up" her intention to remain in school. The earlier the student considers this question of homesickness the better. Let her face its possibilities before she goes away from home, and make up her mind, if she is attacked, resolutely to overcome it. If it comes, let her never give up the struggle, for, by giving in, she will only lose ground in every way, morally, socially, intellectually. By her cowardice she will part with what she can never recover later.

Many temptations follow in the wake of homesickness, and the most serious of all is to make friends too rapidly. It may be laid down as a rule that a friendship formed on this stop-gap principle, and too rapidly, is not likely to endure. Such a friendship is not a sane or a wise relation, for friendship is like scholarship: if it is worth anything at all it comes slowly. Impulsive, quickly forced friendships are not wise investments ; the very fact that they come so quickly implies an unbalanced state of idealizing, or lack of self-control. This does not mean that one is not to form pleasant acquaintances from the very beginning of the school life. Acquaintance-ship always holds something in reserve and is the safest prelude to a deeper and more vital friendship.

There is no denying that there is great temptation to violent admirations and attractions in school. In the first place, in school or college the girl is brought into contact with a large circle of people who are immensely interesting to her. The whole atmosphere is full of novelty, of the unusual. Some of the students and teachers whom she meets for the first time represent a broader experience, it may be, than her own home life has given her. They are often new types and new types are always interesting.

I shall say nothing of the idealism of friendship—it plays its part in other books. It would seem sometimes as if almost too much emphasis had been placed upon the making of friendships in school,—friendship which is, after all, but a by-product, the most valuable it is true, nevertheless a by-product of the life. Wholly practical are the tests of friendship which I shall give. In the first place a friend is too absorbing who takes all of one's interest to the exclusion of everything

else : there should be interest in other people, other activities as well as in one's work.
Such a friendship can only make a girl forget
for what she has come to school.   The new
relation which disposes one to look with less
respect and affection upon one's own people
and home—and they, be it remembered, have
stood the most valuable test of all, the test of
time—cannot be a good influence.   It may be
said in general that an association which is
developing the less fine traits in one's character, giving emphasis to the less worthy sides,
should be relinquished immediately, even at
the cost of much heartache.   The heartache
will be only temporary ; the bad influence
might become permanent.   On the other
hand, since friendship is giving as well as
taking, one does well to consider the fact that
if one's own part in it does not tell for good,
there is just as much reason for stopping the
friendship where it is.   Some of these associations—and this is a hard saying, I know
—which seem everything at the time are

nothing, as the years will prove. A girl idealizes, and idealizes those who are not worthy. Inevitably the day comes when she laughs at herself,—if she does not do worse and pity herself for having been such a goose.

Only a few of the friendships made in school are destined to endure. One of the foremost of those that last is founded on similarity of interest. Perhaps it is the girl with whom one has worked side by side in the laboratory,—a relation formed slowly and on a permanent basis. Many of the best of friends have come together through community of interests, and this is a type of friendship for which men have a greater gift than women.

There is still another type which develops because of some conspicuously noble or fine quality which proves attractive. Hero worship, this, which enlarges one's self through the admiration given to another. Then there is the friendship based on a purely personal attraction, with mutual respect and self-respect as its dedicated corner-stone. This does not mean that one cannot see any faults in the friend, or know that one's own are seen, without losing affection. There is always something flimsy and insecure about a friendship that simply idealizes. Any relation should be all the stronger for a frank acknowledgment of its imperfections. If a girl cares enough she will be willing to admit her own faults and wish to make herself more worthy to be a friend.

And, finally, there is what might be called the lend-a-hand friendship,—the relation that springs into existence because of the need which is seen in another. It is not fair to make a packhorse of one's friend or to turn one's self into the leaning variety of plant, but it is fair and wise and right, if one is strong enough to accomplish the end in view, to lend a hand to another girl who is not making the best of herself.

Have a good time but do not swear eternal

allegiance in this first year to anybody, however wonderful she may seem. Hold yourself in reserve, if for no other reason, then on account of the old friends at home, whether they be kin or no-kin, for they have been true. And remember, as I have said before, friendship is like scholarship and must by its nature come slowly.

IV

THE STUDENT'S ROOM

THERE has been a general improvement in student rooms, yet many rooms to-day have altogether too much in them : too many pictures, too many banners, too much furniture, too many hangings. The great fault of most rooms is this overcrowding. If we were only heroic enough to make a bonfire of nine-tenths of all they contain we should see suddenly revealed possibilities for something like the ideal room.

One serious and obvious objection to the overcrowding of rooms is the hygienic. I am tempted to say that this is the most important objection : indeed, since health is more important than wealth, I will say so. A girl has neither the time nor the ability to keep so many articles in a room clean : and while she is busy attending to her studies, some cherished ornaments are not only laying up dust for the future, as a more regenerate life will lay up treasures, but also breeding germs, perhaps collecting the very germs which will take this girl away from school or college. Besides, bric-à-brac not only gathers dust and breeds germs but also wearies the nerves. It makes one tired to see so many things about, and tired to be held responsible for them. Without realizing it, we resist the amount of space they occupy and in their place want the air and sunshine. Subconsciously, most of us long to get rid of our bric-à-brac and then pull down the draperies that keep out the sunlight. The simpler the window draperies in a room, the more easily washed, the better and more attractive. For wholesome attractiveness there is no fabric that can excel a flood of warm sunshine. Any girl or woman who has curtains which she must protect from strong light by drawing down the shades is guilty of a household sin whose greatness she cannot know. That same sunshine, freely admitted, will do more to cleanse a house than all the soap, all the brooms, and even all the vacuum cleaners ever invented.

The so-called beauty of a room should always give way before the hygiene of a room. Not only should the room be sensibly furnished so that it may have plenty of air and light, but closets should not contain articles of furniture which belong where the air can reach them. There is a difference between a room that is not orderly and one that is not clean. A room that contains unclean articles in drawers or closets, unclean floors, unclean rugs and hangings and unclean walls, should not be tolerated for an instant. If a girl turns a combination bedroom and study in school or college into a kitchen, if an ice-cream freezer occupies all the foreground of this place she calls home, and chafing-dishes with cream bottles, sardine tins, cracker boxes, paper bags full of stale biscuits, fruit skins, dishcloths and grease-spotted walls, all the background, it is impossible to have a clean room to live in.

The Golden Rule applies to rooms as well as to human beings and should read, "Do unto a room as you would it should do unto you." And not only for the sake of health should this Golden Rule for Rooms be observed but also for the sake of the college or school. The room that belongs to us only for a time should be as thoughtfully cared for as if it were our own personal property. There is something inconsistent, isn't there, in educating a girl in high thinking and fine ideals, if she is willing to live in a room that for uncleanliness many a woman in some crowded quarter of a city would consider a disgrace? Such contradiction in mind and surrounding is out of harmony with all one's ideal for a gentlewoman.

Not only beauty is restful, peace-giving and peace-bringing, but so, also, are neatness and order. Orderliness helps to fit one for work. There is undoubtedly some connection between surroundings and one's mental state. In themselves disorder and confusion are irritating. The sight of a dirty child crying in the doorway of an untidy house suggests some connection between the wretchedness of the child and the squalor of the home. I often think of William Morris, the great craftsman and charming poet, who had much at heart the happiness of all people, especially the poor, and his exclamation, " My eye, how I do love tidiness !" To him, to the artist, it was, as it is, beautiful. George Eliot had to put even the pins in her cushion into some neat arrangement before she could sit down to write. Disorder wastes not only one's feelings and health, it also wastes one's time, for a lot of this commodity may be lost in looking for books, wraps, gloves and other things which are not put away properly.

School ought to be a training for the life afterwards. That is why we go to school, isn't it? Why should a girl indulge herself in habits which will make against her usefulness in the life of the home or in whatever circumstance she may be? There is a certain disciplinary value in order. Every great military school has recognized this. Laxness in the care of one's room may mean the habit of laxness in other and more important ways. Disorderliness indicates a certain tendency in character, and if a girl allows that sort of thing to go on she is very likely to show it in other ways. Untidiness in any of one's personal habits—and what could be more personal than a room?—should be taken up and corrected even as one attempts to correct any weak point in one's character.

Do you know what is always—that is, if it is in it at all—the most beautiful thing in a room? It is something which the Creator meant all mankind should have, rich and poor, old and young alike; it is something beyond the buying price of any wealth. It is the sunshine, more beautiful, more valuable than expensive hangings that shut it out. Perhaps it is partly because it is inexpensive, God-given to all people, that housewives frequently draw their curtains against it. If they had to pay more for it than for carpets and hangings, you may be very sure that a great many husbands and fathers would be overworking in order that their families might buy a whole display of sunshine instead of tapestries.

Do you know what is the most helpful thing you can have in your room, the article without which you cannot live in it at all, no matter how fine the rugs and bric-à-brac may be? *Air!* Air is the one thing which is almost instantly and absolutely indispensable to human life, for we breathe it in not only through our noses but also all over our skin. Every hundredth fraction of an inch of our bodies is feeding upon air, and the purer that air and the cooler the better and more invigorating food it provides for the skin surface as well as for the lungs. The mind, for it is housed in the body and its tenant, must depend for its vigour or tone upon the fresh air in school or college study. Even a very good head cannot work well set upon an anæmic body which is suffocating for want of good clean air. If you wish to do your best work and keep well, the first thing to do is not to open your books but to open your windows. After that the books and a reasonable number of hours of continuous study. American audience halls, pullmans, ordinary coaches and public buildings of all sorts, especially libraries, are notoriously over-heated and unventilated. It is the intelligent American girl and woman who, beginning with the home, will correct this evil. The schools are, on the whole, in the forefront of the fresh air movement, especially the public schools. As every one knows, the public schools are establishing open air rooms for their children who need them. Although there is much to be said about what a room should contain to make it attractive, it should never be forgotten that sunshine and fresh air are more beautiful and more priceless than anything else which it can hold.

The first object in furnishing a bare room is to make it habitable,—that is useful. Take the kitchen, for example, and usefulness is practically the sole object in fitting it up. And the curious thing about it all is that it cannot help being beautiful in a homely, motherly way, for it exemplifies one of the strongest elements of all beauty and that is *service*. The kitchen may be a very humble place but if more women would make a study of their kitchens and then take thought, it is likely that the rest of their houses would be in much better taste. A thing that is useful, even as with some well-worn homely old woman who has led a good and helpful life, always acquires a beauty of its own. It may be hard for girls to see this but it is there, and in time it will be seen. Just as it is essentially more beautiful to have a clean, strong body rather than a pretty face and a body that is not what it ought to be, so is it more truly beautiful to have articles of furnishing in our rooms, in study or kitchen, that are of indispensable genuine use.

Take the gaudy ambitious study one girl has made for herself. It is defaced by the presence of articles of no value at all in the world of needs; there is nothing in it that is genuinely beautiful and nothing that is substantially useful. The furniture is almost too cheap to stand on its own legs, and the colours would certainly never wash and not even wear. This room is a junk-shop of new, useless, unattractive objects of no virtue,—in short, a most unpleasant place in which to live. Have you ever considered what gives even the simplest clothes for distinctive occasions a beauty of their own? It is fitness. And it is this same fitness which tells so much in furnishing a room. It might be said of certain dresses that they "go together," that is, they are harmonious, they belong together, they have, like some people, the beauty of agreeing with themselves, and a very desirable sort of beauty it is. Just as clothes are an expression of the people who wear them, so are rooms an expression of the people who live in them. No well-bred girl cares for tawdry, cheap, over-ornamented clothes. She is made uncomfortable even at the very thought of having to wear such things. She should suffer just as much discomfort on the score of a cheaply furnished (and by "cheap" here I do not mean inexpensive—whitewash and deal intelligently used may create a beautiful room), overcrowded and over-ornamented study.

What is the meaning of the room which is your school centre for the time being? It is an intimate place where a girl may have her friends and good times; it is a retreat and it is a workshop. It is the girl's home centre away from home, the place from which she will lead her life, in its expression attractive or unattractive, like her or unlike her. To intend that this room in beauty, in cleanliness, in order, shall be the best expression possible of the girl's best self is the ideal to set for the school study.

Get good materials and good colours. They need not be expensive. Remember that colours have to go together just as furniture has to do so. To have styles of furniture that clash or colours that do not harmonize will negative any care which the student may have taken in the selection of individual pieces or materials. To have too much with which to fill the room is a good deal worse than not to have enough. Much better it is to have a few things which are just what they should be than to have too many and those undesirable. To get a desk, if a girl can afford to do so, that she will be glad to keep her life long is a good beginning, and a comfortable chair that will be made doubly precious by all the school associations woven about it. And let her be careful about pictures for her walls and not crowd them with cheap and "fashionable" trash. Above all, let her remember that good taste, simplicity, careful selection, will do more to assure her the possession of an attractive room than all the money in the world can do.

V

THE TOOLS OF STUDY AND THEIR USE

A GIRL ought to take up her study with the same sense of pleasure as that with which a strong workman enters his shop, knowing his tools and able to use them. Having good tools and knowing them is certainly part of the joy of work. And what are the tools the student must use? Well, for the average student, the one that is first and most important is *Good Health.* The mind is not as clear if the body is not in good health, clean within and without.

The second set of tools consists of a different sort of equipment and apparatus, tools with which a girl must become familiar and which she must know how to use—*Books, Library, Laboratory* and *Classroom.* Why shouldn't a student be just as able to use her books as a carpenter his plane or saw? One couldn't expect a fumbling carpenter or a clumsy seamstress to accomplish much work or good work. There are times when a girl need not claim to know anything but she must, at least, know where to find what she wants to know. This is the first lesson in the use of books ; without knowledge of them or love for them, the student can't get along at all. And beyond this somewhat mechanical use of books there is a deeper and larger lesson to learn ; to know that a book is not merely a page of print where information may be sought but that it is a mirror in which one finds the world, its wisdom, its joy, its sorrow, its divine adventures. Robert Southey, the friend of the poet Coleridge, has written beautifully on the subject in a little poem called " His Books."

Another tool in the student's workshop is *Previously Acquired Knowledge :* that is, what one has in one's mind. Some people's minds are junk-shops. But a junk-shop is better than an empty shop. This previously acquired knowledge, if used rightly, becomes the tool of later courses, the servant of later years. Our stored-up facts—many of them —have not been an end in themselves. How could they be? For example, such things as paradigms and formulæ and long lists of names and dates, are tools pure and simple; but the student in the workshop must have them or she will be like a carpenter who had much to do but on coming to his bench found no tools there and so was idle all day.

A fourth tool for the girl in her study—one that cannot be deliberately acquired, as information or apparatus or even health can be—is *Experience.* This is the most valuable tool of all—one's experience of travel, with people, in responsibility, in love, in joy, in sorrow, in any kind of work. The girls who are the most interesting in the classroom are the girls who are not contenting themselves with apparatus alone but whose minds are flexible with experience, who bring all of themselves, their life, to bear upon the work. A certain well-known minister had prepared a sermon for his usual Sunday engagement, but half an hour before service another text came into his mind. He could not forget it, so he jotted down notes and preached the new sermon instead of the one that had been prepared. This sermon made a great impression on all who heard it, and the minister himself said of it that some people would declare that it had been thought out in half an hour, but that really he had put fifty years of his life into it. The sharper and better the tools, the finer the character of the work. If experience has been observed and retained, and previously acquired knowledge is ready for service, and hand and mind know how to use books, and the student is in good condition physically, then the excellence of that girl's work in the class and out can be guaranteed.

And now what are the uses of the work which these tools can accomplish for us? Coleridge wrote in his poem, " Work Without Hope,"

" Work without Hope draws nectar in a sieve,
And Hope without an object cannot live."

The only hope that can last is hope that **is** not wholly centred in ourselves, but has some thought for others and our service to them. Work devoid of inspiration and ideals, work done merely for one's self, study pursued with only a degree as an end or for the sake of "pay" as a teacher, turns school and college into a market-place, a place of barter, where in exchange for so much energy and so much money we may acquire a certain position and livelihood. Only that work in which one has the consciousness of being, or becoming, useful to others, brings joy that will endure. What do we think of the minister who is without a sense of **consecration**? The responsibility of the student or the teacher is quite as large, the opportunity for service quite as wonderful. One of our greatest English poets, William Wordsworth, exclaimed: " I wish to be considered as a teacher, or as nothing !" The calling of the teacher, of the student, has through all time been thought a high one,—one that has drawn to itself fine and unselfish spirits. The life of the student, no matter how necessary to the world its market-places are, never has been and never can be a life of barter, of trade.

The wealth that comes to the student should not be an exclusive possession. It may be bought at a large price but it can never be sold. It must be given away, or shared, for it is wealth which carries with it a sense of social responsibility. It is enjoyed for a double purpose, not only for the sake of the happiness it brings to us but also for the sake of the joy or help it may bring to others. Millions of girls covet the opportunities that come to a few in school and college, many of them who far more greatly deserve this privilege than we. Indeed, what have most of us done to merit the right to all that we have? The only way in which we can show our sense of justice is by taking our privileges as something to share with others.

The girl who has health, pleasant surroundings and work worth doing, has all a human being has a right to expect. She ought always to be happy, always rejoicing in her work and always eager to divide her wealth with others.

The redeeming feature of royalties has been their sense of responsibility for their subjects! In great disasters, or calamities, their first thought has been to go to the relief of the people. The King and Queen of Italy are noble examples of this courage and unselfishness. In America the only "privileged" class is the highly educated. It is they from whom *noblesse oblige* must be expected, who will show in all emergencies their sense of responsibility, who will share all that they have with others. A girl will be happy, she will grow, she will be a leverage power for good with those among whom she lives, only in so far as she uses her tools of knowledge in the service of others, and shapes all that she does towards some humanly useful end.

VI

THE JOY OF WORK

IF one is in good condition, the exercise
of any physical power is a pleasure. It
is a pleasure to run, to sing, to dance,
to climb mountains, to row, to swim; it is a
pleasure to shout for nothing else than for
the pure joy of letting off surplus energy.
In the world of animals, the horse and dog,
to take only two illustrations, abound in this
enjoyment of physical energy. The horse
paws the ground and snorts and whinnies
and loves the fastest road pace you will let
him take. The dog leaps in the air, jumps
fences, barks, and races around madly, sometimes after nothing at all.

But the highest power of which human
beings are possessed is not the power of the
body. It is the power of the mind. Yet
many of us throughout our school and
college life not only do not wish to use this

power but even rebel against it. " What," some girls are saying to themselves, " enjoy the work of a classroom? Who ever heard of such a thing!" Yes, just that. And if we don't enjoy the work of a classroom, even an indifferently good one, there is something the matter with us, or the subject should not have a place on any curriculum. Every mental exercise should be full of the keenest pleasure, of intellectual pleasure.

Our schools and colleges to-day are very much richer in the joy of everything else— in beautiful surroundings, in freer and fuller athletic and outdoor life, in a more varied and delightful social life—than they were fifty or even twenty-five years ago. But it is a question whether the joy of intellectual work has kept pace with this joy of life in its other aspects. Sometimes it almost seems as if intellectual eagerness were in inverse ratio to the ease and fullness of the opportunities we have. At least many fair-minded girls have seen the predicament in which the teacher is placed. The man who makes a vase for the use and pleasure of others may rejoice not only in his own workmanship but also in the thought of the service and delight he is giving to others. That is, his pleasure is twofold. The teacher who is deprived of some response of joy in the work he is doing is a workman deprived of his rights. To those girls who are thinking of becoming teachers this should be a sobering thought.

Missionary teachers, with their students eager to get anything they have to give, are not to be pitied. Our schools and their groups of teachers in isolated and uncultivated parts of the West and South are not to be pitied. Even if education is with them shorn of much that gives it charm, the opportunities that come are prized. Students and teachers have intellectual joy in the work they do, and without that the greatest university in the world might as well, or better, be a district school, for then the work done would be truly useful.   It is the teacher who has to put much of her time and energy into making a subject superficially attractive enough for a student to elect it, who is to be pitied.   A classroom full of blasé girls whose minds need to be tickled before there is the least expression of intellectual mirth upon their faces, is an ordeal not lightly to be met except by the professional joker or academic tumbler.

Girls often become impatient with themselves, and that is one reason why there is so little joy in work for them.   Think of Helen Keller as a famous example of this joy in work under the most adverse circumstances. What could be greater than her handicap? Shut away from the world by deaf ears and blind eyes and, for a while, by inability to speak, she has nevertheless shown a keenness of pleasure and intellectual acquisition that shames us who have all our senses in their fullness.   Think of her patient, unremitting delving, of the digging up, up, up to get to the light which most human beings are privileged to enjoy with no effort at all! The mind that accepts this wealth with no thought, no sense of responsibility, is a trifler with riches that are about us for God-given purposes. Think of the way in which Stevenson and John Richard Green and George Eliot rose above their ill-health and did their work in despite of it! Perhaps some of us have superb health and have never made any conscious effort to use that gift for a high end.

Girls grow impatient with themselves when they wouldn't be impatient with a little child. Yet the mind has to be trained even as we train a child; it has to be brought back and back, again and again to the thing to be done. After the asking of a simple question, oftentimes a whole class will look confounded, because they have some strange notion that thinking means getting hold of something very far away and difficult to grasp. All that the first effort in thought denotes is taking a hold of that which is nearest and following it up. It is the old story of Theseus following his clue of thread, the slender thing in his hand, by which he was guided out of the labyrinth and to the broad sea of adventure.

There are difficulties in the doing of any work that is worth while. It would be a poor adviser who painted the student's way as a path of roses. First and foremost, one's own inertia interferes with the joy of work. Some one has defined the lazy man as one who doesn't want to do anything at all, and the indolent man as one who doesn't want to do anything that he doesn't want to do. Then, too, there are certain allurements and distractions in school life which are a hindrance to our joy in an intellectual task. And there is the very natural disinclination to the drudgery involved in all hard labour. No work that is worth while is without drudgery. Lack of encouragement from older people is one serious difficulty some girls have to meet.

There is a type of older person who is sure that using the mind will harm that precious article. And, finally, there is our inexperience, our own lack of comprehension, our own purposeless and formless lives.

Joy in work should not be altogether conditional upon one's sense of ease or upon what is called success. Seeming success is not always success. Often the most valuable lessons come from failures. Robert Browning, the poet, speaks again and again of the noble uses of failure. Let me quote one stanza from one of his greatest poems, " Rabbi Ben Ezra " :

> " Then, welcome each rebuff
> That turns earth's smoothness rough,
> Each sting that bids nor sit nor stand, but go !
> Be our joys three-parts pain !
> Strive and hold cheap the strain ;
> Learn, nor account the pang ; dare, never
> grudge the throe ! "

You can't learn to walk if you haven't tumbled down a good deal in doing it. It is often failure that means ultimate success. Of course if a girl keeps on saying: "Oh, what's the use?" about everything she does and all her failures, there isn't any use. In weak moments that sort of thing can be said of every great and worth-while experience, of love, of joy, of sorrow, of work. But a girl who allows herself to take this attitude is a "quitter," and doesn't know the first principles of playing the game.

Part of the joy of work consists in the mere delight of intellectual exercise, delight in thinking a thing out. That is the way we develop ourselves mentally, just as we develop ourselves physically through sports. The mind that thinks is capable of deeper and broader thinking. Thinking begets thought. A muscle that is left without exercise softens and finally atrophies. The same is true of mental muscle. If this strength is left unused it is gradually lost and cannot be recovered. Mental concentration, the thought that is so strenuous that everything else is shut out, strengthens the mind. In this wonderful old world no new land has been discovered without physical effort. There is no country of the mind which can be entered without a similar effort.

And there is another and very important joy in work—the sense that one is being equipped for the work of the world, for usefulness. The mere feeling that one's powers are being developed brings joy with it. There is still another joy which every one of us must covet—the sense of entering into the intellectual riches of the world, its wonders of science and art and letters, with the feeling that we have a part in a great treasure, a treasure which, unlike gold and precious stones, men have never been able to gauge or to exhaust. Such gold and silver as we take from that adventure cannot be lost or stolen from us. It remains with us to the very last, and with it no life can ever become really poor, or dull, or old.

VII

FAIR-PLAY

FEW students realize how closely a class-room resembles a commonwealth. To most of us it seems a place into which we go to have a certain amount got out of us, or put into us. This conception of the classroom is unworthy the modern girl who has, otherwise, a fine understanding of the meaning of team-play, of playing all together for a common end, a game or a republic united by a tacit compact.

Does the average student feel responsibility for the game of basket-ball or lawn hockey which she is playing? The first thought of the girl in answering this is that it was a foolish question even to ask. Of course she does. But for her classroom? No, that is a different sort of game, in which the responsibility lies all on the shoulders of the instructor. It is a one-woman or a one-man game, and very often the students are but spectators, cheering or indifferent, approving or disapproving. The pupil does not hold herself accountable for this game; it is the teacher who makes the class "go," who extracts from each student the information bottled up in her, together, often, with a good deal of carbon dioxide,—a process difficult and hard as drawing a swollen cork out of a soda-water bottle. Finally, with a sort of noble rebound of effort, the exhausted instructor is to put a vast deal of information back into the girl before the student claps her book together and rushes pell-mell to the next classroom, there to be similarly uncorked, if the teacher has learned the art and her mental muscle is sufficient.

Such a conception of a classroom is not fair-play. The teacher, like the coxswain of a college crew, may have rowed over the same course and she may know it well enough to cover it in the dark; she may have won distinction upon it, may be the fittest person in all the states of the Union to cover it again, but if she has not a good or a winning crew to coach, she will never win any race, even the shortest. No instructor has shoulders equal to such a multiple burden as coaching, steering and doing all the rowing, too. To play any classroom game in this spirit is to be dead weight for every one else embarked upon the same adventure. It is not fair-play.

By such an attitude on the part of merely one student in the class, every other student associated with her loses, for the girl who will not lift her own weight the others must carry. If that student were playing in that spirit on the basket-ball team, do you suppose that the coach, or the captain, would let her stay on? Not for a moment; off she would go and very much humiliated, too. If it is a discussion, the touch and go of the whole recitation will depend upon the presence of the team-play, or fair-play, spirit in the course. The instructor may do her best but if there is no play-the-game in that classroom, she might just as well fold up her tent, like the proverbial Arab, "and silently steal away." It is not that any recitation need be a brilliant affair—if most of them depended upon that for existence they would scarcely exist at all—but there must be an honest, earnest, responsible effort to make the best of the hour. Good will inevitably come from the clarifying effort to express thought, and the leading from thought to thought as the work goes forward.

The basket-ball team cannot win, or even play, unless all the members are playing together. Each one is needed despite the fact that she may not be one of the chief or best players. Just so does the class need all its students. If a girl is only average, it is not fair-play for her to sit back and do nothing; neither is it fair-play for her to monopolize the attention if she happens to be more than commonly able. It is not fair-play to laugh at the girl who is at a disadvantage, or to appear bored. It is unfair to the individual, to the classroom in general and to the instructor. The least she can do in this class game is to give her whole and her courteous attention.

Think of all the practice games in which the average athletic team takes part. What can be said for the student who comes into the classroom unprepared to lift her own weight, unprepared to help others? When one comes to think about it from the fair-play point of view there is nothing to be said for her. Nor is it fair-play for a girl to allow herself to get into such a state physically that she is unable to study. How often and often have fudge-heads—due to an application to too much sugar and not to books—sitting row after row killed a school or even a whole college! Before a class tempered by fudge and not by wholesome outdoor living and conscientious devotion to work, the teacher might better put away her notes and close her book. Nothing can happen through or over that barricade of fudge-heads.

And it is not fair-play to cram because of time lost, or for any other cause. The only end of cramming is that the student soon forgets all that has been learned. Alone by normal, slow acquisition and all the associations formed in such learning can information come to us to stay. It may not be particularly wicked to cram if one has plenty of time to waste, but it is foolish unless one has.

There is a kind of gossip in which a girl takes part, made up of snap-shot judgments of the classroom, idle carping about some little unimportant point, expression of wounded vanity and unfair talk, which may mean a tremendous loss of prestige for a really admirable course; it may mean that girls, who would naturally go into it because of their liking or gift for the work, do not go or go in a critical and unsympathetic attitude. If there is a complaint to be made about any course it should be made to the responsible person concerned, and that is usually the teacher. Anything else is not fair-play. In the classroom the instructor is the "coach" of the game and she is the person with whom to talk. It is needless to say that if a girl is putting nothing into a course she cannot expect to get anything out of it, or to complain because things do not "go." If she wants them to "go" why does she not help, and have the profit of taking something away from the work as interest on her effort? A girl gets dividends only from work into which she has put some brain-capital.

And the people at home? Is it fair-play to them, when they are making sacrifices of money or of happiness to keep the daughter at school, for her not to put good work into her study and play her part faithfully in the classroom game? So many things have to be taken into consideration of which we are not likely to think. There is the girl herself, the other girls with whom she is working, the instructor, the people at home, the institution that is providing an expensive equipment or plant through the philanthropic efforts of others or the taxation of the public. If the girl does not play her part fairly, there is a rather big reckoning against her, is there not?

VIII

THE RIGHT SORT OF LEISURE

THE right sort of leisure ought to help as much in the development of the girl as the right sort of work. If it is leisure worthy the name, it will bring refreshment ; it will not leave one physically and mentally jaded. Neither mind nor body should ever be exhausted because of the way in which freedom has been used. Leisure is as important to work as work is to leisure. A person who has not worked cannot appreciate freedom, while the one who has had no leisure is not best fitted for work. "All work and no play makes Jack a dull boy ;" it is just as true that it makes Jill a dull girl. The girl who works all the time, not realizing the importance of free moments, becomes fagged in body and mind. She is a tool that is dull, and would do well to remember that even a machine is better for an occasional rest.

The Right Sort of Leisure

Some mistaken ideas about leisure have grown up, making it difficult to say anything on this subject without being misunderstood. Stories—whole books of them—about "spreads" and more or less lawless escapades in school and college, have given girls and other people, too, the impression that this is the sort of thing school leisure is. Nothing could be farther from the truth. Midnight feasts may occur in school, and most of us, unless we are too good to be average girls, have taken part in them. But such stories are vicious, for they misrepresent the life by suggesting that eating inferior and unwholesome food is the real freedom most girls desire. There is something repulsive in the very thought. Feasts that leave a girl with a coated tongue and a dull head and Monday "blues" do not fairly represent school or college leisure. Good times that interfere with good work have no place in ideally free hours. But, indeed, the odours from the chafing-dishes do suggest that some

of the girls are trying to put into literal ex-
ecution the wish of a great German professor
in Oxford. The professor, eager to try a dish
he saw on the hotel bill of fare, but with his
English and German verbs not quite disen-
tangled, said to the waiter, "Hereafter I vish
to become a Velsh Rabbit." Perhaps becoming a Welsh rarebit represents the height
of some girls' ideals, but this is hard to be-
lieve.

The possession of leisure depends to a
great extent upon the will power. The girl
who has never learned to say " No," who has
no power of selection, cannot expect to have
any hours for her own use. She is quarry
for every idle suggestion, every social engagement, every executive " job " which
pursues her. The girl who engages all her
time socially cannot have a sense of leisure,
for she turns her playtime into but another
schedule, to be met as inexorably as her
academic courses. Her days become a for-
midable array of " dates," often stretching

ahead for weeks. Even if girls are not de-
termined to have it for themselves, they
should give to others some opportunity for
freedom, and should respect their possible
desire for solitude. The girl who engages
or annexes every particle of time, her own or
that of some one else with whom she comes
in contact, is making leisure an impossibility.
The girl who leaves no margin cannot hope
for even the spirit of freedom.

Many students excuse themselves for much
executive work in school and college on the
ground that it is done in their leisure. That
girl is a goose who allows herself through
any sense of self-importance, or irreplaceable
usefulness, to be so involved in executive
work that all other aspects of her school life
are slighted. If she refuses to be swamped
by such "jobs" she can have the happiness
of reflecting that probably some girls who
need the training far more than she does are
doing the work. To every girl will come the
opportunity right along for "managing";

club and social work will bring it, and a good-sized family will bring it as nothing else can. But school leisure she will not have again. The whole aim of the school is to enrich the lives of its students, and it knows all too well that that student who does not keep for herself the leisure upon which body and mind and soul must feed is indeed poor.

There is one way in which leisure is very generally misspent in school—and alas, outside, too!—not in managing one's own affairs, but in managing and discussing the affairs of others. At such times the remarks may be superlatively pleasant, but they are more often superlatively disagreeable. It may be said with truthfulness that they are almost never moderate or just. Everything is all black or all white, with no gray. It makes one think of the little girl with a curl in the middle of her forehead :

" When she was good, she was very, very good,
And when she was bad, she was horrid."

But, alas ! the poor wretches discussed are not

allowed even the natural and somewhat happy human alternation between badness and goodness. No, indeed, they are monsters of a desperate character—they may at the moment be broken-heartedly conscious of their own faults—or they are shining six-winged angels. And, woe ! this sort of thing comes almost as hard upon the angels. They can't endure it ; so much goodness breaks down their wing arches, and the glorious ones crumple together like tissue-paper.

And upon the girls busily engaged in creating angels of loveliness and gargoyles of ugliness, this sort of conversation works havoc. It does not invigorate them, it does not inspire them. It belittles their minds— thank fortune, that making kindling wood of the characters of other people does do this ! —and stunts their finer feelings. This sin, that they " do by two and two," they pay for one by one. Gentle and considerate feelings are lost, time is wasted, a vicious habit,—almost no habit is more vicious,—is acquired.

Such gossip can never become a pure enjoyment; it remains at the best an ignoble, discreditable excitement. Rolling these sweet morsels under their tongues, a taste for ill-natured or exaggerated comment fixes itself in their mouths. Even if they have consciences that, like good mothers, will occasionally wash their mouths out with soap, they retain the disturbing memory of unkind, coarse, or foolish words.

Yet school should be the last place in which to indulge in idle talk. Such indulgence is against all the idealism of student life. Idle or meddlesome talk never helps any one, either the one who talks or the one who is discussed. If you have anything to say about other people, and if going to them will help you, the only friendly thing to do— it is not an easy thing—is to speak to the people concerned. If we really knew how to put ourselves in other people's places, no unkind, unfriendly words would ever be spoken again. There would be things hard to bear said—rebuke or reproof are never easy to receive—but nothing unfriendly. Think how idle, ill-natured talk flows around the world, and then think what a different world it would be if there were none of it! It is to human life what the blights, the scales, the insect pests are to tree and flower. Fortunately, as people grow older they come to think themselves less infallible, and as they grow wiser they become more tender and more lenient in their judgments.

In companionship whose leisure interests are good there is a sense of freedom filled full and running over, of minds and hearts doubly rich, of good times doubly jolly. But on the whole, girls have too little absolute solitude; there is scarcely a girl in twenty, except the "dig," who is alone at all. One trouble with dormitory school life is that it fosters leisure-wasting and time-wasting "gang" habits. A girl so surrounded never wants to be alone a moment, either indoors or out. With such, the blessing and blessedness of solitude should be learned, for solitude rightly used makes strong men and women.

The woman who has leisure has a grasp upon time, is master of it instead of being mastered by it. It is the girl whirled around in a squirrel cage of pointless weekly and Sunday engagements who is oppressed and mastered by her lack of freedom. And then there is the hard-pressed future; we must lay up some leisure for that. The time when one is most hurried is the time when one most needs the sense of freedom. The story of the old Quaker lady who had so much to do she didn't know where to begin, and so took a nap, is profoundly full of wisdom. When the old lady woke up she found she had plenty of time after all, not because she had done anything but because she had come again into a leisurely frame of mind.

Leisure means neither a blank mind nor an empty hand. It means a holiday taken with an eager mind, with eyes keen in their delight and knowledge, with hands capable of some beauty or some use. All of us have leisure to think, but not all of us think. Some of us, if friends come in unexpectedly, will quickly pick up something and pretend to be busy. When Watt sat by the fire watching the steam from the teakettle lift the lid, he was not precisely idle. The powerful, indispensable steam-engine was the result. One reason, aside from all religious considerations, why we need a quiet Sunday, is that we may have that sense of freedom which feeds mind and body, and even the crumbs of whose profitableness have made the world rich in great inventions, in great pictures, in wonderful books.

IX

THE OUTDOOR RUNWAY

AFTER Nebuchadnezzar came in from eating grass there had taken place in that potentate a great change for the good. One of the factors in this betterment may have been the grass itself. The grass-cure has always been popular and always will be, for it is just as good for the tired mind as it is for the tired body. Nowadays every big school and every college provide a grass-cure for students who are out at elbows with their nerve sleeves, or who have not sufficient muscle to make them fit, or who are overworking or need toning up in any way. There is more and more recognition of the fact that a school course which is taken at the expense of health is not worth having. And side by side with this wholesome admission has come a great awakening in the last fifteen years to the curative value of the *outdoor runway,* whether that runway be a field track, energetic walking in a park or campus, or a cross country run.

Some girls—and there are more girls of this type than there are boys—put in their outdoor life as a stop-gap. It is inconceivable that this should be true, yet it is true. Apathetically the students have exercised sixty minutes, considering this minimum quite sufficient. Not a particle of zest do they reveal in the exercise taken. They do not seem to know or they do not care that the fields and woods should be full, not only of health and all that goes with it, including success, but also of the best of friends who all have their good points worthy of notice and imitation, in quick leap, cheerful voice and blithe song. What are sixty minutes in this great outdoor runway? Not a tithe of the twenty-four hours and at best only half of what the minimum should be. Exercise should be taken even if nothing else in the school life is. And I say this advisedly, for health is the basis on which not only the future of the woman's life must depend but also that of the race. Good health, the inheritance of it, its maintenance and increase, neither the girl nor her parents can ever hold as too sacred a trust. That it is a sacred trust the schools are recognizing more and more, and provisions are being made, especially in the public schools, for the defective in health as well as for the strong. The outdoor school, at first an object that attracted universal attention, is now being taken quite for granted. Foolish the girl who does not learn to take the outdoor runway for granted, too, and go out to it in high spirits to learn its wisdom, to take part in its joys and to receive its health.

It may be accepted as a new axiom—the more exercise the less fool. Strong, able muscles, steady nerves (and let us remember that nerves depend for their tone on the muscular condition), a clean skin open at all its pores and doing its eliminative work thoroughly, and clean strong vitals make up the kind of beauty within the reach of all womanhood, and the physical beauty which she should most desire. The day is coming when our ideal of what is physically perfect —not spiritually, for Christianity has carried us beyond anything that Greece ever knew —will be more like the Greek in its entirety, its emphasis upon the harmony of the whole body. The body is a mechanism to be exquisitely cared for—self-running, it is true, and yet in need of intelligent attention. Think of the care an engineer gives his engine, and it is by no manner of means so wonderfully and so intricately fashioned as these bodies of ours on which our happiness, our working ability, even our very goodness depend. Health as a safeguard to one's whole moral being is coming into more and more recognition, and not only as a safeguard but also as a cultivator of all that is best in us spiritually. There are people very ill, or permanent invalids, whose great victory it is to be among the saints of the earth, but that it is easier to be good when one is well no one will deny. Every big school has now its class or classes in corrective or medical gymnastics, in which stooping shoulders, ewe necks, curved spines, flat insteps, small waists and narrow chests are rectified as far as possible in the limited hours of the school days.

The time is coming when parents will consider it a disgrace to allow their children to be physically undeveloped. The physician, always in advance of the community for which he cares, sees how grave in moral or intellectual import physical defects may be. The educational world, alive to new messages for the reconstruction of its educational ideal, begins also to place more and more emphasis upon the physical care and development of its students—and not by any manner of means for physical reasons only but because the whole girl or the whole boy is better spiritually and mentally for having a body that is strong and well. The whole being keeps better time, just as a watch does, for having clean works. No one has the right to shut out the fresh air or the sunshine; no girl should remain undeveloped physically through lack of exercise when she could, through exercise, make herself strong. Even to abuse her feet, the important centre of many important nerves, by tight shoes, is wrong; so is it to rack her spine and upset or throw out of position all the delicate and wonderfully fashioned organs of the abdominal cavity by the wearing of high French heels. Undoubtedly, however, American motherhood and girlhood represent something more and more intelligent; indeed, in physical culture women are beginning to keep step with men, and it is upon this fact that school and college depend in their splendid efforts to make the sum of feminine vitality, despite the pressure of modern civilization, plus rather than minus.

The more exercise the less fool; and it is worth remembering that the daily exercise, the plunge into cool or clean air, as well as the plunge into water, is a wit sharpener, and will do more for a student in the long run than "digging" possibly can. *Mens sana in corpore sano* may be an old saying but it is still new enough to be repeated with vigour to certain people. Let us get out-of-doors and have our wits sharpened and see more, and do more, and be more! No one can permanently starve her whole body for the want of fresh air and exercise, which are the body's birthright, and expect to have a clear head or do well-balanced and helpful work in the home, or in school, or in some wage-earning career. If the girl attempt this impossibility she will be like the frog which jumped up one foot and fell back two. She will get to the bottom soon enough, the bottom of the class or the bottom of her health account, but she will never get to the top of anything. Any success, if by chance it should come to her, resting on a basis of ill health or indifference to her physical fitness for living and working, will be like the house built upon the sands. Before the girl is twenty, before she is twenty-five—the earlier the better—she should recognize this fact and begin to establish her life on the bed rock of health.

It is true, too, ninety-nine times out of a hundred, that the country boy and the country girl are more resourceful than their city cousins. Out-of-doors they have had to use their wits and have not been spoiled by all the appliances of city life. Out-of-doors, too, they have made invaluable friendships with bird and squirrel and rabbit and deer, friendships whose intelligent wood-life has taught them much. Self-reliance is one of the lessons of the outdoor runway; and wisdom and inspiration come from it when they are needed. About this truth the work of the poet Wordsworth is one long poem. Again and again he writes of the perfect woman shaped by the influences of nature. Of her he says :

" Three years she grew in sun and shower;
  Then Nature said, 'A lovelier flower
      On earth was never sown;
  This child I to myself will take;
  She shall be mine, and I will make
      A lady of my own.

" ' Myself will to my darling be
  Both law and impulse : and with me
      The girl in rock and plain,
  In earth and heaven, in glade and **bower,**
  Shall feel an overseeing power
      To kindle and restrain.

" ' She shall be sportive as the fawn
  That wild with glee across the lawn
      Or up the mountain springs;
  And hers shall be the breathing balm,
  And hers the silence and the calm
      Of mute, insensate things.

" ' The floating clouds their state shall lend
  To her; for her the willow bend;
      Nor shall she fail to see
  Even in the motions of the storm
  Grace that shall mould the maiden's form
      By silent sympathy.

" ' The stars of midnight shall be dear
  To her; and she shall lean her ear
      In many a secret place
  Where rivulets dance their wayward round,
  And beauty born of murmuring sound
      Shall pass into her face ! ' "

No one can afford to neglect all the spiritual influence of nature, and the only way to receive it is to go to nature. Purity of mind, a clean conception of God's creative plan, a more active intellectual life are all there for the girl who will seek them. She cannot afford *not* to go back to nature for these helps, for every woman is in some sense a burden bearer, and she must needs know all she can of what life means in order to bear these burdens well.

There are various kinds of outdoor life, some one of which is within reach of every human being, even if they are cripples. Probably most girls when the outdoor life of school and college is spoken of think that athletics is meant. That is one part of the outdoor runway, and since it is provided in every school, and insisted upon, but little about it need be said. It is doing its work with more and more inspiration, as the response to its ideals comes in. And it does something more in every well-equipped school than merely make a girl use her legs and arms : it gives her a large, sane ideal of health and provides her with the means of keeping well. There is no more useful profession for the woman seeking one that is useful as well as remunerative than physical culture.

There is another aspect of the outdoor runway of which less is said. I mean gardening, or the care of live stock of some kind, or bee culture. This is practical remunerative work which for the girl living at home and going to school should serve famously as a grass-cure; it would keep her out-of-doors with profit to both her health and her purse. And then there is another kind of grass-cure : the outdoor life out-of-doors, to be taken in long country walks, in fishing expeditions, in picnics, in camping or wherever roads, hills, meadows and brooks lead. Finally, there is the outdoor life indoors. This life insists upon windows open to the air and open to the sunshine, and this life every one of us may have all the time.

X

A GIRL'S SUMMER

ANY girl who settles down to a summer with the idea of doing nothing, or in an aimless, not-knowing-what-to-do-next fashion, lessens her opportunities for pleasure. Pleasure is not idleness, although in the minds of a great many people who have not thought very much it is. The right sort of leisure is full of opportunities for doing interesting things.

There are some girls who look upon their summers as an escape from the slavery of their school year. There are others who think of their summers as something to be endured until they can go back to the more or less selfish freedom of the school. Neither is the right way. The summer ought not to be an entirely frivolous season, neither ought it to be too workaday. If a girl has work to do, everything should be so arranged as not to deprive the vacation of its recreative side.

On the other hand the summer should be all the happier because of a definite object to be accomplished. Something is wrong with a girl unless she finds both summer and winter full of opportunity and pleasure.

No one can possibly do all the delightful or useful things which may be done in a single summer. In these months there is opportunity for growth just as in the winter —perhaps more opportunity physically. And intellectually there is much to be seen and observed. For the girl who can, it is well to plan to be out-of-doors as much as possible. For some, there are opportunities for camping, for long walks, for gardening, to learn how to do certain physically useful things, to row, swim and ride. Only an extraordinary emergency would deprive a girl of all the out-of-door exercise which she needs. If she isn't able to be by the sea or in the mountains, in almost all cities there is opportunity for exercise and games. With a short car ride she can go to golf links, to tennis courts, into the country. In many semi-citified homes there is space for a girl to do some gardening, one of the most profitable of pleasures, good for the girl and good for the home. Many homes would be much more attractive if there were more of the garden spirit in them. But if there is no chance for this, there can always be physical culture, an opportunity to build one's self up in health, to live sanely and wisely, to get plenty of sleep, and to take corrective exercise. In physical culture a girl should find out what she most needs—almost any gymnastic instructor in school or college would be glad to outline work—and then in ten or fifteen minute exercises develop herself along those lines.

For the girl with means there is the chance for travel, a splendid opportunity to cultivate many virtues of which the young traveller seldom thinks : patience, adaptability, seeing the bright side of things. Travelling may be made a very important part of education. It is too bad that some people of limited horizon take it simply as a chance to aggrandize themselves, something to boast about and with which to bore their friends by repeated accounts of what they did " abroad." The great Doctor Samuel Johnson, the compiler of the famous dictionary and author of " Rasselas," heartily disliked young travellers, for, he said, "They go too raw to make any great remarks." Travelling, if it is what it should be, is an educational opening. In this way can be gained a background for history, for literature, for sociology, and a vivid and living knowledge of geography. Merely running about with a guide-book will not achieve these ends, although a guide-book is a very important asset : sympathy, trying to understand what one sees, will. Travelling takes away provincialism because it broadens the outlook. In a very real sense the world becomes one's home.

The girl who is not able to move about or actually travel may travel in books. She should be ashamed to read what is harmful or merely cheap, but further than that it may not much matter. Let her read the Little Books, if she wishes, and the Great Little Books. As surely as the magnet swings towards the pole will the Great Little Books take her to the Great Big Books. She will be drawn on and up in her reading, and will have cultivated a love for reading which is far more important than perfunctory knowledge of the classics.

Just as any books that are good point towards books that are better, so should the good work of a girl's school year be turning her mind towards the future and her work as a mature woman. In the summer she has time to assimilate all she has done, to get her bearings, and to plan wisely for the year, or years, to come. For a girl of strong physique the summer vacation gives an opportunity to add towards what she is going to do eventually; to specialize in some line of work, to take a library, or scientific, course. Many girls, however, who wish to spend their sum-

mer in this fashion ought not to consider it,
for they are not strong enough. It is well for
them to remember that it is the quality of
work that counts rather than the quantity.
Often the quality of a girl's work for an en-
suing school year depends upon her freedom
from study during the summer. Students
should be very sure, if they undertake work
in the summer, that it is not done simply from
a nervous desire to go on regardless of the
quality of the work done. But for those in
perfect health this is an opportunity to try
their powers in different ways in order to dis-
cover what it is they really wish to do. A
summer so spent may keep many a girl from
slipping into teaching just because it seems
the only thing she can do. Such a salvation
will be twofold, for it will save not only the
girl, but also a profession overcrowded with
loveless followers. There are so many needs
to be filled by a woman's work that it is her
duty to look for some vocation for which she
is truly adapted, to get out of the ruts of those

professions into which women flock because they have no initiative.

Often a girl thinks only of what she will do with her own summer without thinking of what she will do with her mother's or her father's summer. For nine or ten months they have been thinking of what they could do for her. Sometimes girls do not realize the actual need of help and of companionship which those at home feel, and the older people are too unselfish to force this need upon their juniors. Between the unselfishness of those who are older and the self-centredness of those who are younger, there is often sad havoc made in a home. A girl who, after a year's absence and all that has been done for her, can't adjust herself to those who need her, has still something to learn.

If older people cannot do without the buoyancy of the young, the young cannot very well afford to forget the mother and father who have much, although no word may be didactically spoken, to teach them. Let the girl take her summer not only as an opportunity to grow closer to her family but also as a chance to learn home-making, to train herself in the practical things of the home. This practical training is often a very valuable supplement to the school work. The time is passed when the learned woman who is unable to do anything for herself is the ideal —if she ever has been that. The inability to make a home for herself, to do all the necessary things daintily, detracts from a woman's power. In practical ways a woman should be both dainty and capable. Parents, as well as girls, sometimes forget or do not clearly recognize the fact that no school, no college, can take the place of the home, that schools are not primarily schools in home-making, but rather schools of general education. The summer is a good time for the girl to find her place again in the home life, and for both parents and children to rejoice in the pleasures of the home—pleasures and opportunities which no institutional life can give.

XI

FROM THE SCHOOL TO THE GIRL

WHAT the school is able to do for the girl depends very largely upon the girl herself. The majority of people with whom she comes in contact do not take that into consideration, and the school is held unfairly responsible for the girl. All any school can do is to use the material it finds. Some one has said, with harsh but true emphasis, that a college does not make a fool, it simply helps in the development of one. As an illustration of its limitations, a school sends out two girls from the same class; one girl it is proud to have taken as a type, the other it is sorry to have represent it. Yet both have been under exactly the same influence. Students do not realize how fearfully at their mercy a school is, or that, so far as reputation is concerned, it is they who make or mar its credit.

If the school training is worth anything at all, it makes the most of unpromising material. Its really discouraging experience is not with the girl of limited ability who gives her best and so in some sense gets the best, but with the student who doesn't give her best and who, because of her own indifference, is always misrepresenting the training she is receiving. No school ever wishes to have its ideals confused by a vulgar display of wealth or by loud or conspicuous behaviour. Yet many a school, with ideals all that they should be, is misjudged in public places because of some thoughtless or unreliable girls. This doesn't seem like fair-play or team-play, does it? The fineness of life ought to be felt and expressed in student behaviour. Yet how often it is not!

Another way in which the ideals of a school or college are misrepresented is by lack of intellectual integrity. Any school informed with a large spirit wishes to meet its students on a platform of absolute trust,—a platform

which makes precautions against dishonesty
unnecessary. Just so long as a school must
be vigilant in order to keep a few students
from unfair behaviour, just so long is it pre-
vented from meeting them all on a basis of
absolute trust. Why should girls excuse
themselves for classroom dishonesty? What
would they think of a girl who cheated in
basket-ball? Would they condone that?
Until student government has recognized
absolute intellectual integrity as a part of its
ideas, it will not have achieved its end. The
rock on which all scholarship is founded is
honour. Lack of honour is fatal to its ideal.
"Cribbing," often excused by people who do
not stop to think, is the small beginning of a
big evil.

Many a large institution is like an anxious
mother, not always infallible in wisdom, but
personally interested in and eager for the
success of the individual. A successful girl
brings credit to her school, for she demon-
strates, as nothing else can, the fact that the

school is achieving its purpose in service to the community. How much this encouragement is needed, girls do not realize, for they do not know all the difficulties which institutions, especially technical and collegiate, have to meet in sending their students out into the world. In finding a position for a student, the school has to consider the whole girl. It may care greatly for an attractive personality and yet see that its possessor is lacking in qualities of faithfulness and accuracy, and that with its utmost endeavour it has never been able to correct these faults. On the other hand, the school may have those students whose manners, whose dress, whose personality, whose spelling, whose awkwardly expressed notes, whose lack of promptness, make against success in any capacity.

Another point for which the school looks in recommending its students is physical fitness, which shows itself in many different ways: in voice, in carriage, in attractiveness, in staying power. One teacher who had an excellent record as a student and was, besides, a fine girl, had so unpleasant and absurd a voice that her students were in a continual state of amusement and would learn nothing from her. A great many teachers have lost in power because of a poor voice, strident, or lifeless, or husky, or falsetto. A poor enunciation, or words that do not carry, are ineffectual means by which to reach a class, to hold a customer, or to introduce one's self favourably to the interest of others. For a girl who is going to have any part in public life—and most girls do nowadays—a good voice is an absolute essential. And it is well for us to remember that the voice is not something superficial, but that it is the expression of that which is within.

Another way in which physical fitness shows itself is in the carriage. A girl who carries herself with erectness and energy brings a certain conviction with her of fitness for many things, of self-respect, of ability, and reveals in her bearing something of her mind as well as of her body. We are always tempted to think a person who "slumps" physically may slump in other ways. A good carriage, good voice, and strong, clean, digestive system are far more important than beauty of features.

There is another matter at which the school in placing its students must look. To be a desirable candidate for a good position a girl need not be expensively gowned, but she must be daintily and freshly dressed. Immaculate shirt waist, a plain, well-made skirt, with good shoes, stockings and gloves and a quiet, pretty hat, are all any woman needs in meeting her business obligations. And that daintiness which she shows in her dress she must show in her person too, in clean skin and finger-nails, good teeth, and smooth, attractively ar-ranged hair.

It is very important for the interests of a

school, as well as for the individual, to place its students advantageously. To have them succeed widens its sphere of usefulness and influence and opens new channels of service. Every college puts itself to considerable expense in looking out for the interests of its students, for the glory of a great school lies not only in the people whom it collects into its midst, but even more in those whom it sends out. A girl has no right to go so lightly through her school life that she fails to see in it all the self-sacrifice and effort and ambitions that have gone into the building up of what is her privilege and opportunity. In so far as she does this she fails in the team-play spirit. Why should a girl think that she can spend her father's money, or the means of her school, thoughtlessly? What would happen to her if she did this with the funds of her basket-ball team? Yet girls waste the resources of their school by carelessness with its property, a carelessness that collectively mounts up into thousands of dollars, and never once stop to think how difficult every big school finds it to make ends meet.

Before it is too late, at least now that she is leaving school, let her stop to realize that a great deal of the work for an institution is along the line of self-sacrifice, in the gifts given, in the work of its administrators and teachers. This unselfishness means a financial loss, for business ability might be invested in more lucrative ways; it means a social sacrifice, for there is a certain kind of impersonality which is demanded in work that deals with a continually changing community; it means risk in the great strain put upon physical and nervous strength; it means forgetting one's self; for the true teacher is willing to be forgotten when she has served others. What a school may accomplish for its students is its only compensation for all this self-sacrifice.

XII

THE WORK TO BE

ONE of the qualities a girl who has completed her school or college life needs to show for a few months more than anything else is the quality of adjustment, for she will find that she must continually adjust herself to new conditions whether they be of the home or elsewhere. All the time through school she has been in some sense a centre of interest. Her class has been an important factor in the academic life. When she has gone home it has been as a school or college girl, and she has been of interest because she brought that life into the home. But now the attitude of others towards her is different. She ceases to be the centre of attention, and for her a day of serious readjustment is at hand. Perhaps in her own estimate she has seemed even more important than she really was. She is likely now to swing from a sense of self-importance to an injured feeling of insignificance, and to a conviction that people can get along quite as well without her. Up to this time when she has gone home she has been an honoured visitor. But now that she is at home to stay, instead of becoming the centre she is merely part of the family circle with its obligation of doing for others. Her presence in the household is no longer a novelty.

The swift change from a highly-organized, methodical life to the life of the home where there is not so much method, is hard for a girl. One reason it is difficult is that while she may be accomplishing a great deal that is useful, she seems to be doing nothing and to get nowhere. She feels as if she were in the midst of a conflict of duties. In school she has had implanted in her the idea that she must accomplish some definite thing, and between this objective and the irregular demands of the home there appears to be more or less clashing. She is confronted by a problem not easy for any one to solve : how to keep her definiteness of aim and work, and yet not be self-centred.

Oftentimes when a girl fails to adjust herself to the home life, her family and friends feel that she is rather selfish in her desire to carry out her own aims rather than to give them up for new demands. Frequently the family is as much to blame for not realizing that the girl needs to be helped back into the old life as the girl is for not being able to help herself. In the home the spirit of team-play is much needed. Quite as much as the girl, the family has a lesson to learn in the art of adjustment and in remembering that this grown-up child isn't just the same individual she was when she went away several years ago. They need to realize that the girl may be able to give more to the home life than she ever did before, but that it will be given in a somewhat different way.

While she is learning the difficult art of finding her place again, a great deal depends upon the individual girl, not only in the home but in the community at large. Sometimes she needs to be reminded that although she may have had more advantages than those left at home, that doesn't necessarily make her a superior person. A girl who is inclined either to pity or to admire herself too greatly should give herself a vigorous shaking. In the long run she will find it easier to do that on her own account than to have others do it for her. The friends at home, or in the church, or in the town, with education of a different kind coming to them, may have quite as much and more to give her than she to give them. One indicator of a really cultivated woman is her power to adapt herself to the circumstances in which she is placed. A gentlewoman never calls attention to the difference between herself and somebody else. The woman of broad culture is the one who makes everybody feel at home with her. If a girl's education has been worth anything at all, it should give her not a superior, set-aside feeling, but a desire to be more friendly and useful wherever she may be, and, not placing too much stress on externals, to look for essentials, to get the full value from every person and from every experience with which she comes in contact.

Girls go to so many different kinds of homes that it is unlikely that they will meet the same sorts of difficulties. There is the girl who goes into the society home, where it is impossible for her to carry out her ideals without conflict with its social standards. On the other hand, there is the girl who goes into the very simple home where all the stress is upon the domestic side of life. And there is the girl who has to provide part of the family income. Very likely she has the hardest problem of all. She enters upon some new work, and nine times out of ten the way is not made easy for her; she is a novice with all the hardships that come to the novice. Perhaps in the beginning she has met a very real perplexity in hardly knowing what line of work to take up. She has no particular interest, no especial talent, no brilliant record, no powerful friends, no money with which to establish herself. With her it must be as it is with thinking : she must seize hold of the thing nearest her. What seems to her a temporary and unsatisfactory expedient will in many cases open out a path leading to something much broader. At least she may remember this as consolation : that even that experience of uncertainty, of indecision, is a part of education, and out of it, rightly and bravely met, will come some richness for her future life.

The beginning of a work, teaching or anything else, may have to be rather irksome, indeed, may be exceedingly difficult,—an experience that will perhaps test staying power to the utmost. When it is too late to give due appreciation we realize that the work in school which was planned for us and arranged with our physical and mental well-being in view was, after all, not so hard as we thought it at the time. We wish that we had enjoyed our leisure more and complained less.

From the point of view of fatigue, as a secretary, a clerk, a trained nurse, a teacher, a social worker, the burden may be so great that the girl is disheartened. She is all the more disheartened because, knowing that a useful life is a strong, steady pull, the way before her seems interminable. If she carries her whip inside her—this counsel is not for those of us who are lazy—she does well to remember that there is a point beyond which fatigue should not be borne, that is, when it overdraws her capital of health and nervous energy. Raising pigs is preferable to a so-called high profession when pig-raising is happily joined with a reasonable amount of health and security. The pigs and health together can always pay mortgages and buy necessities for those dependent upon us and for ourselves. The high calling without health is like a wet paper-bag : it will hold nothing.

The girl meets with another difficulty in finding out that in almost any line of work a great deal of time is needed for the mastery of what seem the simplest principles. No one wants the girl who hasn't had experience, and nobody seems disposed to take her and give her that experience. However, we all find some one who is hardy enough or kind enough to try us; and as every year now there is more effort put into finding the work girls are most suited to do, there is no excuse for slipping into teaching as a last resort. Not unnaturally we sometimes distrust ourselves, especially in taking up an occupation to which we are not accustomed. And in her new work the girl, uncertain of her ability to master what she has undertaken, is placed in a position in which she has the encouragement of neither the school nor the home. Before, she has put much of the responsibility for her work and life upon parents and instructors. Now she has to be her own judge and pass judgment on herself and her work. She has, too, not only to lift her own weight but the weight of others as well. As she longs for coöperation, good will and encouragement the value of the team-play spirit has never seemed so great before.

We do not need to be told to remember the happy and easy experiences of life. No girl forgets them. What we do need is some one to tell us where the hard places will be, to warn us, to stiffen our courage and to point clearly to the uses of hard work and adversity. And although this may seem like placing another straw on the poor camel's back, it is now time to say that in her life-work, whether it be in her home or outside, a girl should be very clear in her mind what her aims and purposes are. If she is working solely for the praise and commendation of others, she will often be grievously disappointed. Not in recognition does real reward lie, but in the work itself. If she wins great popularity she is likely to find that there is nothing that shifts so quickly and is such a quicksand. If material wealth is her sole object she will harden into the thing she seeks and add but another joyless barbarian to a modern world congratulating itself that barbarism is a thing of the past, and yet presenting the spectacle of a mammon worship such as has never been seen before. If gold is her end, and not the means to a nobler end, then she will find herself constantly sacrificing higher issues to that, and lowering her one-time ideals. Truly the woman who marries solely for the comforts of a home, the woman who teaches, or nurses for "pay" alone, has her reward, and that is in self-destruction. She is a carrier of barbarism, not of culture ; of disease, not of health ; of tribulation, not of joy. The only real reward there can be lies in the idealism, the joy, the strength of the work done and in a mind and heart conscious of having done their best.

THE END

JOHN T. FARIS   *Author "Winning Their Way."*

"Making Good" Pointers for the Man of To-morrow

12mo, cloth, net $1.25.

Dr. J. R. Miller says: "Sixty intimate messages to young men and boys on the things that make for success or failure. Bright and short and full of illustrations from actual life, they are just the sort that will help young men in the home, in school, among associates and in business. Everywhere is the suggestion of the necessity for Christ if men would build up fine character and make life worth while."

JEANETTE MARKS, M. A.

A Girl's School Days and After

Introduction by Mary E. Woolley, President of Mt. Holyoke College. 12mo, cloth, net 75c.

In twelve most readable and suggestive chapters ranging from "The Freshman Year" through "School Friendships," "The Students Room," "Tools of Study and Their Use," "The Joy of Work," "The Right Sort of Leisure," "The Girls Outdoor Life," to "The Work to Be," the author writes in a practical yet interesting way of wellnigh every phase of the girl and her school.

FREDERICK LYNCH   *Director of N. Y. Peace Society.*

The Peace Problem The Task of the Twentieth Century

Introduction by Andrew Carnegie. Cloth, net 75c.

Andrew Carnegie commends this book in no stinted terms. "I have read this book from beginning to end with interest and profit. I hope large editions will be circulated by our peace organizations among those we can interest in the noblest of all causes."

JAMES M. CAMPBELL, D.D.

Grow Old Along With Me

12mo, cloth, gilt top, net $1.25.

"Shows in most helpful fashion things one should strive for and guard against, things he should leave off doing, as well as others he should put on. It is a pleasant thing to read and it should be a potent factor in leading one to an appreciation of the real beauty and opportunity that lies 'west of fifty years.' "—*Chicago Tribune.*

MRS. NEWELL DWIGHT HILLIS

The American Woman and Her Home

12mo, cloth, net $1.25.

The author shares with her gifted husband the power of both entertaining and influencing people with the pen. The remarkable interest awakened lately by Mrs. Hillis' articles in "The Outlook" has inspired this helpful book.

WILFRED T. GRENFELL, M.D.

Down North on The Labrador

Illustrated, 12mo, cloth, net $1.00.

A new collection of Labrador yarns by the man who has succeeded in making isolated Labrador a part of the known world. Like its predecessor the new volume, while confined exclusively to facts in Dr. Grenfell's daily life, is full of romance, adventure and excitement. The *N. Y. Sun* recently said: "Admirable as is the work that Dr. Grenfell is doing on the Labrador coast, the books he has written, make his readers almost wish he would give up some of it to write more."

CLARA E. LAUGHLIN

The Gleaners

A Novellette. Illustrated, decorated boards, net 75c.

Again Miss Laughlin has given us a master-piece in this story of present day life. Millet's picture, "The Gleaners," is the moving spirit of this little romance and, incidentally, one catches the inspiration the artist portrays in his immortal canvas. "The Gleaners" is issued in similar style to "Everybody 's Lonesome," of which the *Toronto Globe* said: "One of the successful writers of 'Good Cheer' stories for old and young is Miss Laughlin, and whoever reads one of her cheery little volumes desires more."

PROF. EDWARD A. STEINER   *Author of "The Immigrant Tide," etc.*

The Broken Wall

Stories of the Mingling Folk. Illustrated, net $1.00.

Professor Steiner has the story-teller's knack and uses his art with consummate skill in this collection, where will be found dramatic tragedy and profound pathos in strong contrast with keen humor and brilliant wit, all permeated by an uncompromising optimism. No man has probed the heart of the immigrant more deeply, and his interpretation of these Americans of tomorrow is at once a revelation and an inspiration: a liberal education in brotherhood.

A. D. STEWART

Heather and Peat

12mo, cloth, net $1.20.

"This is a very delightful story, told in the broadest and most fascinating Scotch language. The author belongs of right to that class of modern Scotch writers who bring out matters of vital human interest, with religious and tender touches, and this story is one that any writer might be proud of and any reader of feeling and vitality must delight in."—*Journal and Messenger.*

YANG PING YU

The Love Story of a Maiden of Cathay

Told in Letters from Yang Ping Yu. Finely decorated boards, net 50c.

Written in English picturesquely colored with Chinese, at once naive and yet full of worldly wisdom, frank and yet discreetly reserved. The story as told in the letters is real, vivid, convincing. It is a human document that will compel the attention of the reader from beginning to end, and verify again the saying that "truth is stranger than fiction."

MARION BLYTHE

An American Bride in Porto Rico

Illustrated, 12mo, cloth, net $1.00.

"The story is very pleasant and very human. In her bravery and courage, in her wit and merriment, the bride reminds one somewhat of the "Lady of the Decoration." This similarity adds, however, rather than detracts from the charm of the book. She is thoroughly good-natured and clever and companionable, with a whimsical and ever-present sense of humor."—*Chicago Evening Post.*

ISLA MAY MULLINS

The Boy from Hollow Hut

Illustrated, 12mo, cloth, net $1.00.

Readers of John Fox, Jr.'s stories will recognize the location of this story at once. The author and her husband, President of the great Theological Seminary of Louisville, have taken a large interest in these descendants of *some of the best American stock.* Through the tender humanness of her narrative Mrs. Mullins bids fair to gain a large audience for this intensely interesting work.

DR. OLIVIA A. BALDWIN

Sita, A Story of Child-Marriage Fetters.

12mo, cloth, net $1.25.

A realistic story of native and mission life in India; a story dealing with the stress of famine and the pathetic condition of India's child-widows.

MRS. MAUD JOHNSON ELMORE

The Revolt of Sundaramma

With an introduction by Helen B. Montgomery. Illustrated by Gertrude H. B. Hooker. Net $1.00.

Sundaramma, a Hindu maiden, is the heroine of this story which relates her revolt against child marriage and her flight from such slavery.

NORMAN DUNCAN *Author of "Dr. Luke," etc.*

The Measure of a Man

A Tale of the Big Woods. Illustrated, net $1.25.

"The Measure of a Man" is Mr. Duncan's first full-sized novel having a distinct motif and purpose since "Doctor Luke of The Labrador." The tale of the big woods has for its hero, John Fairmeadow—every inch a man whom the Lumber Jacks of his parish in the pines looked up to as their Sky Pilot. Human nature in the rough is here portrayed with a faithfulness that is convincing.

ROBERT E. KNOWLES *Author of "St. Cuthberts," etc.*

The Singer of the Kootenay

A Tale of To-day. 12mo, cloth, net $1.20.

The scene of action for Mr. Knowles' latest novel is in the Crow's Nest Pass of the Kootenay Mountains of British Columbia. To this dramatic field he has gone for local color and has taken every advantage of his wide knowledge, picturing life of every phase in his most artistic style.

HAROLD BEGBIE *Author of "Twice-Born Men"*

The Shadow

12mo, cloth, net $1.25.

A new story by the novelist whose study of regeneration, "Twice-Born Men" has made the religious world fairly gasp at its startling revelations of the almost overlooked proofs of the power of conversion to be found among the lowest humanity. His latest work is a brilliant study of modern life which will maintain the author's reputation.

RUPERT HUGHES

Miss 318

A Story in Season and out of Season. Illustrated, 12mo, cloth, net 75c.

"Is there any excuse for one more Christmas story?" "Surely nothing has been left unsaid." "The truth, perhaps." "The truth?—about Christmas! Would anybody care to read it?" "Perhaps." "But would anybody dare to publish it?" "Probably not." "That sounds interesting! What nobody would care to read and nobody would dare to publish, ought to be well worth writing."

J. J. BELL *Author of "Oh! Christina!" etc.*

The Indiscretions of Maister Redhorn

Illustrated, 16mo, cloth, net 60c.

The thousands who have read *Wullie McWattie's Master* will need no introduction to this Scottish 'penter" and his "pint o' view." The same dry Scottish humor, winning philosophy and human nature fairly overflow these pages.

CPSIA information can be obtained
at www.ICGtesting.com
Printed in the USA
BVHW071714031218
534659BV00015B/508/P